S0-AYG-274

SANDRA FRIEND

FLORIDA

Illustrated by

LAURA FRANCESCA FILIPPUCCI

❦ Charlesbridge

WELCOME TO FLORIDA!

When you think of Florida, you probably think of sunshine, beaches, and vacations. It's true that, as the southernmost state in the continental U. S., Florida gets plenty of sunshine. It has 1,200 miles of coastline, so you're never far from a beach. Millions of people visit Florida on their vacations. But there's more to Florida than sun and beaches.

Florida's name comes from the colorful wildflowers that grow everywhere. When Ponce de León came here in 1513, he called the land "La Florida," the land of flowers.

Florida is not a new land—it rose from the sea after the time of the dinosaurs. Ancient tribes lived along rivers and coastlines. They made canoes from cypress logs. Florida's earliest people lived here for thousands of years. But then the Spanish, French, and British arrived in the 1600s. They built cities and missions, and drove off the native peoples. The ancient ways of life vanished forever.

Florida bursts with natural diversity. There are tropical jungles, hundreds of crystal-clear springs, and dark brown rivers that bubble like cola. There are animals and trees found nowhere else on earth! Come take a journey through this land of sunshine, and learn what Florida is all about.

PENSACOLA: FLORIDA'S WESTERN GATE

Pensacola hides treasures in the water. Divers examine the U.S.S. Massachusetts, America's oldest battleship. After it was too old for service, the U.S. Navy used it for target practice, sinking it in 1921. Now it's a home for sea urchins, starfish, mussels, and grouper.

Three forts protected the city. Waves washed Fort McRae into the sea. But Fort Barrancas and Fort Pickens still stand. Imprisoned in Fort Pickens in 1886, the Apache chief Geronimo had hundreds of curious visitors daily.

The Florida National Scenic Trail starts at Fort Pickens. It ends 1,300 miles later in the Big Cypress Preserve. Hikers walk through forests and marshes, and along prairies and beaches.

Pensacola was founded in 1569 by Spanish explorers. Later, French citizens built beautiful homes with wrought-iron balconies. During the American Revolution, the British claimed Pensacola. Confederate soldiers held the city at the start of the Civil War. The flags of Spain, France, Great Britain, the Confederate States, and the United States still fly over Pensacola's city hall, as a tribute to the city's rich history.

In Pensacola, the white sand beaches look like sugar and the sea sparkles. Ancient live oak trees grow along the shore at the Naval Live Oaks Preserve.

PANHANDLE PLACES

At the Apalachicola Bluffs and Ravines Preserve, you can follow your nose to the Florida torreya tree—its other name is the stinking cedar.

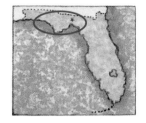

More endangered red-cockaded woodpeckers live here than anywhere else in the world. They drill homes in living longleaf pines. The pine tree must be at least 100 years old for the woodpecker to choose it for a home.

On a map it looks like a frying pan handle. But to the people who live in Florida's long and skinny Panhandle, it's a cool place. White sand dunes rise in front of Destin. People play at Panama City Beach. The Apalachicola River bluffs at Torreya State Park provide Florida's widest scenic view. Fort Gadsden, built by the British during the War of 1812, once protected the river from invaders.

When water erodes limestone, it makes a strange landscape called karst: rock full of holes, cracks, and crevices. A big hole in karst is a sinkhole. A hollow in karst is a cavern. Karst holds water like a sponge, creating a reservoir known as the Floridan Aquifer. Most of Florida's fresh water comes from this aquifer.

At Falling Waters State Park, the state's tallest waterfall drops 70 feet into a dark sinkhole. In Florida Caverns State Park, plump stalactites dangle from a cavern ceiling.

TALLAHASSEE: THE CAPITAL CITY

Tallahassee, Florida's capital, started in the wilderness. It's a hilly place, with dark woods and bubbling streams. In ancient times it was an Apalachee village. Spanish missionaries came here in the 1600s. They built one of their first Franciscan missions, San Luis de Apalache, and tried to convert the native peoples to Christianity. In 1704 the British attacked. They burned the mission and the village. The American colonies were brand new, and the British feared that the Spanish would attack their new colony of Georgia. Tallahassee, chosen because it sits halfway between busy St. Augustine and Pensacola, became the state capital in 1824.

Visitors walk through the Museum of Florida History. It's a place to learn about the Apalachee and other early cultures of Florida. Climb aboard a replica steamboat. Learn about Florida's role in the Civil War. The Florida Agricultural Museum shows off frontier farming. It explains the naval stores industry, which relied on tapping Florida's pine trees for turpentine and rosin to make wooden boats waterproof.

Every 25 years Lake Jackson disappears! The fish—and everything else in the lake—drain into a sinkhole, and then slowly the lake fills back up again. Lake Jackson Mounds Archaeological State Park preserves an ancient village from A.D. 1000–1450. Six earth temple mounds are part of the village. Archaeologists have found tools, burial objects, and pottery shards.

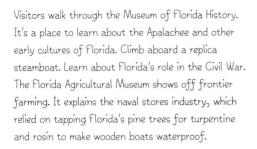

Florida's first railroad ran from Tallahassee to St. Marks. Now a rail trail follows the route. Near its end is the St. Marks National Wildlife Refuge. Alligators laze along dikes. Herons poke through the shallows. In the fall, the shrubs blaze orange—but not from leaves. Thousands of monarch butterflies rest here on their migration to Mexico.

THE SUWANNEE RIVER

Stephen Foster's song "The Swanee River" brought attention to this long, winding river through North Florida. It starts in the Okefenokee Swamp in Georgia and flows 265 miles to the Gulf of Mexico. At the northern end, tupelo forests crowd the shore. At Big Shoals, canoeists carry their canoes around the rough white water. The lower Suwannee is a land of cypress swamps. Manatees winter in the warm, clear waters of Manatee Springs.

In Osceola National Forest, walk the Nice Wander Trail to see red-cockaded woodpeckers. Their pine tree homes are marked with bright white bands.

The Suwannee flows into the Gulf of Mexico near Cedar Key. The Cedar Key State Museum shows off local history, including huge iron kettles used to boil sea water into salt. In the 1860s, Cedar Key was a boomtown thanks to a factory that made cedar trees into pencils. But in 1896 a tidal wave from a hurricane wiped out houses and factories. Now the scattered islands are part of Cedar Keys National Wildlife Refuge.

The Olustee Battlefield Historic State Park is the site of Florida's largest Civil War battle. More than 10,000 soldiers met here on February 23, 1864. Every February reenactors set up a Civil War encampment at this park.

The town of White Springs was founded as a spa along a spring in the river. Above the old spa is the Stephen Foster State Folk Culture Center. Every May the Center hosts the State Folk Festival.

The Forest Capital State Cultural Museum in Perry presents Florida's logging history. Longleaf pine and cypress became boards and boxes; sand pine, mashed to a pulp, turned into paper. Timber companies today rely on the fast-growing slash pine.

GAINESVILLE AND OCALA

Bison and wild horses roam at Paynes Prairie Preserve State Park, a vast wet prairie that 1700s botanist and explorer William Bartram called the "Great Alachua Savanna." In the 1800s Florida cowmen drove their cattle across the prairie. The cowmen were called Crackers for the sound of their bullwhips over the herd. If you walk along the prairie, watch your step! Thousands of snakes, lizards, turtles, and alligators call Paynes Prairie their home.

Florida's first national forest was the Ocala National Forest. It protects the world's largest sand pine scrub. Within the Big Scrub you'll find dozens of bubbling springs. Florida's rarest creatures live here—the Florida scrub-jay and Florida sand skink.

Silver Springs is the world's largest freshwater spring. It pumps out 834 million gallons of water a day—enough for a city of three million people! In the 1920s movie studios made Tarzan movies along this jungle-like forest. Watch out for the monkeys! Rhesus monkeys, left behind by the movie people, live along the river.

Home to the University of Florida, Gainesville attracts students interested in the natural world. They study zoology, botany, agriculture, veterinary science, and medicine. Caretakers watch after endangered fruit bats at the Lubee Center. The Florida Museum of Natural History shows off Florida's wealth of fossil discoveries. There are mastodons and mammoths, rhinoceroses and three-toed horses, saber-toothed tigers and bear-dogs. Students visit an 1890s farm at the Morningside Nature Center. A newer farm is at the Marjorie Kinnan Rawlings homestead in Cross Creek. She lived here in the 1940s and wrote her novel *The Yearling* here.

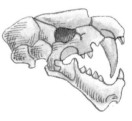

CENTRAL HIGHLANDS

Orange blossoms fill the air with their strong fragrance. Most of Florida's oranges and grapefruit come from Polk County.

Reenactors gather at Dade Battlefield State Park and at Fort Cooper State Park to remember the Second Seminole War.

When Spanish explorer Hernando de Soto came to Florida in 1539, he wanted gold. He landed at Tampa Bay and marched north with his men. He never found his treasure. But in the early 1900s, explorers found phosphate—a great fertilizer. The phosphate boom brought settlers to this hilly part of Florida. They founded the city of Inverness along Tsala Apopka Lake and settled many smaller towns, too, like Dunnellon. At the south of the phosphate belt is the Mulberry Phosphate Museum. Florida is still the top source of phosphate in the United States.

Rangers take care of injured birds and manatees at Homosassa Springs State Wildlife Park. "Mermaids" swim at Weeki Wachee Spring, as they have since 1947. These actors learned how to perform underwater between breaths from air hoses.

The Florida Pioneer Museum at Dade City explores life on the Florida frontier. Nearby Withlacoochee River Park has a restored Cracker village and a Creek Indian village. The park lies on the edge of the Green Swamp. It's more like a forest than a swamp. It has pine flatwoods, dry sandhills, and cypresses.

The Withlacoochee State Trail runs through Inverness. It provides bikers a 43-mile paved path from Dunnellon to Dade City. The Withlacoochee State forest is Florida's largest state forest, with caverns, rivers, sandhills, and swamps. People come here to camp, hike, canoe, and ride horses.

THE SUNCOAST

Along the Suncoast, cultures mingle. Sponge beds in the Gulf of Mexico attracted Greek sponge divers, who founded the town of Tarpon Springs in 1876. Tarpon Springs attracts tourists. They enjoy the Greek restaurants and gift shops. Coastal Dunedin looks like a seaside Scottish village. It has shady narrow streets—and wild parakeets! Flocks of green monk parakeets flutter overhead. Their grandparents escaped from birdcages. Just off the coast between the two cities, pelicans and ospreys build their nests on Honeymoon Island.

At the tip of Tampa Bay, Fort de Soto stands guard. It was built for the Spanish-American War, but the soldiers at the fort never fired a shot. Visitors enjoy the beaches and campground. They canoe through the mangroves and hike under the sea grapes.

On the south shore of Tampa Bay is the city of St. Petersburg. It was one of the land boomtowns of the 1880s, and its long pier is one of the oldest in the country. It's a city of museums: the Salvador Dali Museum, the Museum of Fine Arts, and the Tampa Bay Holocaust Museum.

The Clearwater Marine Aquarium lies on the bayside. Volunteers rescue stranded and injured dolphins, sea turtles, and manatees, bringing them here to rest. At the Lowry Park Zoo, stingrays wait to be petted. Florida panthers pace back and forth. Busch Gardens shows off animals of the African savanna. It's also a great place for roller-coaster rides. The nearby Museum of Science and Industry has IMAX films and interactive exhibits.

In Tampa they celebrate pirates! Jose Gaspar was one of the last Spanish pirates. His pirate ship attacked Florida vessels until 1921. Every February "pirates" play at attacking Tampa during the Gasparilla Festival.

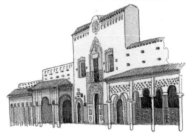

Old Cuba lives on in Ybor City. It's an old-time Tampa neighborhood with Havana flair. Cigars were once the industry of Ybor City, but it's now more popular for its Cuban restaurants.

THE SOUTHWESTERN GULF COAST

The enormous Ringling Museum of Art is in Sarasota. It's Florida's official state art museum. Circus showman John Ringling collected fine art from Europe. He also opened the world's largest display of circus memorabilia.

There are more seashells on the shores of Sanibel and Captiva Islands than anywhere else in the country! The Bailey/Matthews Sea Shell Museum shows off shells plucked up after storms.

The Southwestern Gulf Coast is a place for beachcombers to play. Sea oats wave atop sparkling sand dunes. The shallow Gulf of Mexico shimmers with stingrays and horseshoe crabs. Coconut palms shade many beaches. At Longboat Key, sea turtles lay their eggs. When the babies emerge they scoot to the sea. On Sanibel Island everyone looks for colorful seashells. Birdwatchers come here, too. They like to spot rare white pelicans, mangrove cuckoos, and roseate spoonbills at the Ding Darling National Wildlife Refuge.

The Gamble Plantation Historic State Park is South Florida's only remaining antebellum (pre–Civil War) home. It was once a 3,500-acre sugar plantation.

Little Salt Spring near Fort Myers holds clues to ancient Florida. Underwater archaeologists found human bones and tools thought to be up to 12,000 years old. The Madira Bickel Mound holds more clues. Here, archaeologists discovered three different periods of Indian cultures. The Calusa were one of the fiercest ancient peoples. They paddled their canoes from island to island in the Gulf. They lived atop shell mounds and built canals. When the Spanish came in 1513, the Calusa fought for their lands. They left Ponce de León with a fatal wound but eventually were defeated.

THE EVERGLADES AND BIG CYPRESS

At Fakahatchee Strand, delicate ghost orchids bloom in the trees.

Think pink! As you approach Flamingo, watch for flamingos. Bright pink roseate spoonbills roost in the mangroves.

In 1947 the writer Marjorie Stoneman Douglas called the Everglades the "river of grass." It's a unique landscape—part swamp, part forest. Before man tamed the land, the shallow river seeped in a miles-wide sheet from Lake Okeechobee. But dikes and canals slowed the flow. Now sugarcane grows around Florida's largest lake. The Everglades shrank but did not die. It is one of the wildest landscapes in America. Lone cypresses rise from thick foggy mists. Vast prairies of razor-sharp sawgrass stretch to the horizon. Tall forests of cypress are draped in orchids, ferns, and Spanish moss. Because Spanish moss is an air plant, it needs no soil to survive. Hundreds of different kinds of air plants live in the Everglades.

Long Pine Key is one of the last pine rockland forests in Florida. The delicate ferns and flowers here only grow on bare limestone. Developers and farmers have blasted apart these limestone islands throughout South Florida.

Everglades National Park encompasses most of the Everglades. A tram ride into the wild departs from Shark Valley. The Main Park Road to Flamingo leads past hiking trails into the "river of grass."

During the Third Seminole War, the Seminoles who did not surrender fled to the Everglades with Chief Billy Bowlegs. Two separate tribes formed. Their descendants, Miccosukee and Seminole, live on scattered reservations along the edge of the Everglades.

Florida panthers slink through Big Cypress. There are fewer than 100 remaining. Related to the southern cougar, they once roamed all of Florida. As settlers created farms, the panthers were killed or fled south.

THE FLORIDA KEYS

A jewfish slides past a diver. These huge spotted fish can grow up to 685 pounds! Relatives of the grouper, jewfish enjoy the sea around Fort Jefferson. But you can see one in the Key West Aquarium, near Mallory Square.

The tiny Key deer—the smallest deer in North America—chew on mangroves for food. There are fewer than 300 of these endangered deer remaining. Less than three feet tall and 65 pounds, they risk their lives crossing the road. Most of them live on Big Pine Key in the National Key Deer Refuge.

The fragile Florida Keys are America's tropics. They stretch like a string of pearls from the peninsula, connected by the Overseas Highway. Transparent blue water surrounds each island, and tropical fish flutter through the shallows. The Florida Keys National Marine Sanctuary protects the nation's largest living coral reef. Parrotfish and stingrays slip through chambers of coral. John Pennekamp Coral Reef State Park provides a place to snorkel or scuba. The Jules Undersea Lodge is a hotel on the ocean floor!

Tropical plants from the Caribbean thrive in the Florida Keys, creating miniature jungles on rocky soil. Look for colorful tree snails climbing the speckled bark of pigeon plum, and rare white-crowned pigeons eating the fruit of the dangerous poisonwood tree.

The Overseas Highway, linking Miami with Key West, opened on July 4, 1938.

Two fortresses protected this "Gateway to the Gulf." At Fort Taylor, archaeologists discovered Civil War cannons buried in newer buildings. Fort Jefferson lies 70 miles west, on one of the tiny islands of the Dry Tortugas. It's a popular spot for diving and snorkeling.

The southernmost city in the United States, Key West was founded in 1826 by shipbuilders and wreckers. Artists and writers love it here. Ernest Hemingway left behind an unusual legacy: the descendants of his six-toed cats stroll around the Hemingway House. Wild roosters roam the streets of Key West, colorful blurs in the tropical sun. At sunset everyone goes to Mallory Square. Jugglers and acrobats show off their stuff as the sun sinks into the sea.

THE SOUTHEASTERN COAST

More than 700 wild animals roam the Miami Metrozoo. With its open-air exhibits, the zoo is one of the nation's top zoological parks.

At the Marinelife Center of Juno Beach, researchers rescue and rehabilitate sea turtles.

Today's Miami is a hip melting pot of Hispanic culture. It all started in 1896, when Henry Flagler pushed his Florida East Coast railroad south to Fort Dallas, a quiet trading post on the Miami River. When the railroad came, the population boomed. Farmers grew citrus and pineapple in newly drained marshes. Attracted by Flagler's elegant hotels, wealthy visitors came from New York and Europe. Caribbean and Latin American immigrants came looking for freedom and fortune. Miami's population exploded in 1959 when Fidel Castro took over Cuba. More than 400,000 Cubans sought refuge here from communism. They passed through the Freedom Tower, called "Miami's Ellis Island."

First illuminated in 1860, the red brick Jupiter Inlet Lighthouse still signals to ships. Climb the dizzying spiral staircase for a sweeping view.

The place to see and be seen is Miami's South Beach. Pastel-colored 1930s Art Deco hotels sit along the shore.

Elegant homes and hotels line the waterfront in Palm Beach. Rich and famous guests still stay at the Breakers, one of Henry Flagler's original hotels. Whitehall, Flagler's residence in West Palm Beach, shown above, lets visitors step back into the Gilded Age.

Southwest Eighth Street is the heart of Little Havana, bustling with marketplaces and restaurants. Every March the community hosts Calle Ocho ("Eighth Street"), the largest Hispanic celebration in the United States.

INDIAN RIVER LAGOON

More than 4,300 animal species live here, including hundreds of dolphins, sea turtles, and manatees.

Where the lagoon meets the sea, sharks appear—from harmless nurse sharks to dangerous great white sharks. Shark attacks are on the rise everywhere along this coast.

The Indian River Lagoon is a ribbon of salt water, stretching 150 miles from Jupiter Inlet to Ponce Inlet, along Florida's Atlantic Coast. The mangrove forests are crucial to the health of the lagoon. In 1903 President Theodore Roosevelt established the very first National Wildlife Refuge at Pelican Island. The refuge is a smattering of tiny islands in the lagoon, near Sebastian Inlet. Pelicans raise their young on these islands.

New Smyrna dates back to 1768, when Scottish physician Andrew Turnbull started the colony. He brought 1,200 servants, men and women from Minorca, Italy, and Greece. They constructed canals and planted rice and indigo. It was a hard life—many became sick and died. After 10 years the survivors gave up and walked to St. Augustine to start new lives.

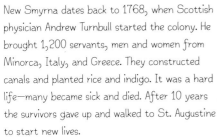

At the National Astronaut Hall of fame, you can meet the people who made history, or learn to be an astronaut-in-training at Space Camp.

In the 1960s a new colony appeared along the lagoon—astronauts! Millions watched Alan Shepard become the first American in space in 1961. NASA's Kennedy Space Center is a very busy place. Today you can watch a space shuttle launch or tour the rocket garden and exhibit halls.

Bird-watchers enjoy winter trips to Merritt Island National Wildlife Refuge. Its marshes and canals provide a winter home for thousands of migratory birds. On the beach side of the lagoon, protected lands form the Archie Carr National Wildlife Refuge. Sea turtles lay their eggs here along undisturbed sands.

ORLANDO

In a blur of blue, a florida scrub-jay swoops over the trail—and onto your head! These rare birds flourish at Lyonia Preserve, a scrub habitat in Deltona.

Downtown visitors stroll around Lake Eola and feed the ducks. In Winter Park, slow boats drift between the chain of lakes.

It was once a quiet town of cattle ranches and orange groves. Now Orlando is all about theme parks—Walt Disney World, Universal Studios, and Sea World. Visitors from all over the world arrive to spend a week or two in these popular "worlds." But Orlando offers a lot more. Founded in 1835, Orlando became a cultural center, with Rollins College and the Morse Museum of American Art. The museum houses the largest collection of Tiffany glass in the country. There are IMAX movies at the Orlando Science Center.

Never, ever call them cowboys. Florida's Cracker cowmen once rode the range between Lake Okeechobee, Lake Kissimmee, and Fort Myers, driving scrub cattle to market. At Lake Kissimmee State Park visitors can watch a reenactment of a day in the life of an 1870s cowman. Cattle ranching remains a part of Central Florida life. Every spring and fall, thousands come to St. Cloud for the Silver Spurs Rodeo.

At Big Tree Park in Winter Springs, the Senator towers over the cypress forest. This huge tree is thought to be 3,500 years old. It's one of many grand old cypresses protected by Spring Hammock Preserve.

Florida's scrub is a dry, desert-like environment. The Lake Wales Ridge is the oldest land in the state. When the rest of Florida was under water, the ridge formed an island—parts of which now stand 300 feet tall. The Lake Wales Ridge is one of North America's most diverse biological communities, with unique plant and animal species.

It's always Christmas in Orlando! Federal troops started building Fort Christmas on December 25, 1837, during the Second Seminole War. Thousands of Christmas cards arrive here annually to get the special Christmas postmark.

THE ST. JOHNS RIVER

During the Civil War a Confederate torpedo sank the gunboat *Maple Leaf*. It lay buried in river mud for more than 100 years until divers discovered the wreck. It's full of artifacts, such as dinnerware and dice. You can see its contents at the Museum of Science and History in Jacksonville.

Steamboats provided a vital link between river towns, carrying supplies and mail. They brought tourists to far-flung destinations like Silver Springs and Sanford.

It's odd for a river to flow north, but that's what the St. Johns does! It's Florida's longest, deepest, and broadest river. When Jean Ribault sailed into the "River of May" on May 1, 1562, he claimed Florida for France. The small French Huguenot settlement at Fort Caroline lived in peace with the Timucua. But in 1565, Spanish soldiers overpowered the French. They destroyed the colony. The Spanish renamed the river the San Juan, which became the St. Johns. The St. Johns seeps north from marshes near Vero Beach. It's called the "River of Lakes" because it flows through many wide lakes. It completes its 310-mile journey past Jacksonville, flowing into the Atlantic Ocean. Jacksonville is the biggest city on the St. Johns River.

Three Timucuan totem poles were found in the mud off Hontoon Island—the only totem poles in America found outside the Pacific Northwest. At Hontoon Island State Park, you can hike to a gigantic Timucuan midden. It's a prehistoric garbage heap of oyster shells and fish bones.

Built in the 1790s, Kingsley Plantation sits along the fort George River near the mouth of the St. Johns. Remains of slave cabins line the entrance to this national park.

More than 100 manatees spend each winter in the warm waters of Blue Spring, just south of Hontoon Island. These unusual sea-going mammals weigh more than a ton. They nibble on water hyacinths, water lettuce, and eelgrass. They spend their summers in the Atlantic Ocean and in the Indian River Lagoon.

THE FIRST COAST

At Bulow Creek State Park, pause under the shade of a 2,000-year-old tree. It would take at least eight people holding hands to circle the base of the magnificent Fairchild Oak.

Founded in 1565 and continuously occupied since then, St. Augustine has a truly international feel. Many of the city's oldest buildings are of coquina, an orange limestone made up of crushed seashells. The Spanish quarried it from Anastasia Island and used it to build homes in the Spanish Quarter. A giant cross stands above the site of the Mission Nombre de Dios, the first mission the Spanish established in the New World. At the St. Augustine Alligator Farm, baby herons perch in trees. Wood storks, herons, and egrets nest above the alligator ponds. They appreciate the protection from egg-stealing raccoons.

Silent ruins stand at Bulow Plantation Ruins State Park, a testament to one of Florida's oldest industries: sugar. Built in 1821, the Bulow Sugar Mill was one of the largest in Florida. Crushed and processed sugarcane became raw brown sugar here. Raiding Seminoles burned the plantation in January 1836.

The Castillo de San Marco is made of coquina. This massive fortress, dating back to 1695, protected St. Augustine from attacks by sea.

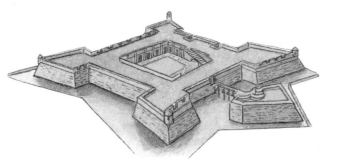

On the Talbot Islands, a painted bunting streaks by—Florida's most colorful bird. It nests in the maritime forest along the coast.

In 1904 Mary McLeod Bethune used milk crates for desks for her new school, the Daytona Normal and Industrial Institute for Negro Girls. As the first free daughter of a slave family, she felt strongly about education. Her school became Bethune-Cookman College in 1923. In 1936 she became the first black woman to head a federal agency, as the director of Negro Affairs.

Two worlds meet at Daytona Beach: the roar of engines and the crash of ocean waves. In the early 1900s, jalopies sped down the beach to inaugurate the first Florida auto races. Today the Daytona 500 draws more than 150,000 racecar fans each February.

THAT'S FLORIDA!

It's more than you knew. It's more than you expected!
Florida isn't just sunshine, beaches, and vacations.
There are alligators and crocodiles, manatees and scrub-
jays. There are mangroves and torreya trees, sea oats
and longleaf pines. There are sand dunes and ridges, long
rivers and deep sinkholes. From Pensacola to Key West,
it's a melting pot of cultures and natural habitats. Florida
is about history and geology. It's about plants and animals.
So much to see. So much to learn. That's the Florida
I know!

RESOURCES

Books

To learn more about Florida's wildlife and history, check out the following books:

Florida in the Civil War: A State in Turmoil by Sandra Friend. Brookfield, CT: Twenty-First Century Books, 2001.

The Florida Water Story: From Raindrops to the Sea by Wendy A. Hale, Jean Barnes, and Peggy Sias Lantz. Sarasota, FL: Pineapple Press, 1998.

Journeys with Florida's Indians by Kelley G. Weitzel. Gainesville, FL: University Press of Florida, 2002.

The Manatees of Florida by Bill Lund. Mankato, MN: Bridgestone Books, 1998.

Panther, Shadow of the Swamp by Jonathan London, illustrated by Paul Morin. Cambridge, MA: Candlewick Press, 2000.

People of Florida by Bob Knotts. Barrington, IL: Heinemann Library, 2003.

Sinkholes by Sandra Friend. Sarasota, FL: Pineapple Press, 2002.

Uniquely Florida by Bob Knotts. Barrington, IL: Heinemann Library, 2002.

Welcome to the River of Grass by Jane Yolen, illustrated by Laura Regan. New York: Putnam Publishing Group, 2001.

The Young Naturalist's Guide to Florida by Wendy A. Hale and Peggy Sias Lantz. Sarasota, FL: Pineapple Press, 1998.

Web Sites

The Internet is an excellent place to find out more about Florida. Remember that Web sites can change, though, so try running a search on your favorite search engine.

http://dhr.dos.state.fl.us/kids/
Check out Florida Kids, presented by the Florida Division of Historical Resources. It links you to cool info on shipwrecks, museums, ancient history, and more.

http://www.flsenate.gov/kids/home.html
At Online Sunshine for Kids, learn all about Florida's capital with information from the Capitol.

http://floridafisheries.com/kids/funstuff.html
Funstuff for Kids serves up wildlife-oriented games and puzzles for kids from the Florida Fish and Wildlife Conservation Commission.

http://www.floridajuice.com/floridacitrus/kids/
Have fun in Florida Citrus Land, the official Web site of the Florida Department of Citrus.

To Amber, who loves Florida. Thank you for your help!
— S. F.

To my children, Anna, Francesca, and newborn Giovanni
— L. F. F.

Text copyright © 2004 by Sandra Friend
Illustrations copyright © 2004 by Laura Francesca Filippucci

Published by Charlesbridge
85 Main Street
Watertown, MA 02472
(617) 926-0329
www.charlesbridge.com

Library of Congress Cataloging-in-Publication Data
Friend, Sandra.
Florida / Sandra Friend ; illustrated by Laura Filippucci.
    p. cm.
Summary: Introduces the diverse places, animals, plants, and people of the Sunshine
State, from the centuries-old homes and forts of Pensacola to the tiny Key deer that chew
on mangroves on Big Pine Key.
ISBN 1-57091-444-3 (reinforced for library use)
ISBN 1-57091-445-1 (softcover)
1. Florida—Description and travel—Juvenile literature. 2. Florida—History, Local—
Juvenile literature. [1. Florida—Description and travel. 2. Florida—History, Local.] I.
Filippucci, Laura, ill. II. Title.
  F311.3.F75 2003
  975.9—dc21   2003003736

Printed in Korea
(hc) 10 9 8 7 6 5 4 3 2 1
(sc) 10 9 8 7 6 5 4 3 2 1

Illustrations done in watercolor and ink on Arches paper
Display type set in Greco Adornado; text type set in Monotype Baskerville;
    caption type set in Argenta, designed by Robert Schenk
Color separated, printed, and bound by Sung In Printing, South Korea
Production supervision by Linda Jackson and Brian G. Walker
Designed by Susan Mallory Sherman